To Cut a Long Story Short...

Kiran.R

Illustrated by Vaseem Sherief

Ukiyoto Publishing

All global publishing rights are held by

Ukiyoto Publishing

Published in 2022

Content Copyright © Kiran.R

ISBN 9789360165635

www.ukiyoto.com

Author's Note

Dear Reader…

Thank you for opening this – my first – collection of stories.

By definition, the essence of flash fiction or 'the very short story' is in powerful brevity. The challenge therein is to create the effect of a story told, without the luxury of length, the comfort of a traditional start-finish-end or the generous use of characters, dialogue and literary devices.

As you read each piece, please remember that it is a small portion of an interesting flavor rather than an enormous and elaborate meal!

Hope you enjoy reading my work…

Kiran.R

This book is dedicated to my wonderful life partner and two extraordinary teachers of English.

Thank you, Mrs. Rugmini Sasidharan (Kendriya Vidyalaya, Kanjikode)

Thank you, Dr. Rama Krishnasayee (Hindustan University, Chennai)

Thank you, Ruchita Jani Kirankumar (Kiran's heart, wherever he is!)

Contents

Torn

He had already seen me. Out of instinct I held my breath and froze all movements – an instinct born out of months of civil war. But I knew he had seen me before I disappeared under the bed. I could smell the outdoors in his boots. I could hear the commotion in the corridor. And I could feel the love in the room. He knew it was me…even the glimpse of my torn shoes was enough for him to recognize me. I saw him walk around stamping his feet, overturning a broken bookshelf, a makeshift table and an old laundry basket. I feared…I wondered…then I understood. He was pretending to search the room. After a minute or two he left.

Voices outside. Two voices; one raised, angry and echoing with the thirst for blood – the other obedient, halting and choking with confusion. Snatches of foreign words that had become all too familiar in the recent past. A few I recognized…*enemy, kill, for our leader, not their country anymore…*

He came back into the room. This time I could only smell hatred. This time I could only see the dead-calm steps of his boots. This time I could only hear the stone-cold silence of his heart. He was in love. But this time, he was on duty.

Gene(rali)talia

Gallery buzzing with soft music and the intelligentsia of the city. The ones who specialize in art, artists and artifice.

My piece GENE(RALI)TALIA is the obvious stunner of the evening. I can hear an important critic's grudging compliment – *the most original artistic idea in years*!

People flock around me. Congratulate me. Pump my hand.

Admirer 1:   *First and only one of its kind. Brilliant!*

Admirer 2:   *Look, you know how I destroy young artists to pieces in my column. But just read what I have to say on Sunday. It's been a long time since I reviewed true art. It's marvelous!*

Admirer 3:   *Stunning idea! With this work you're now a hero to the so-called "different" ones. As an openly gay man, I can assure you!*

Admirer 4:   *What about gender fluidity? Imagine the energy and hope that this gives to people who are forced to live in identity crisis because of stupid heteronormativity!*

Admirer 5:   *Trust me, I have been depicting the human body in my work for seventeen years and this idea never came to me. Fusing the male and female genitalia in such a way that the organs are seen as blended and yet separate. What a bold expression of deviant aesthetics!*

I try not to show my joy and accept the high praise with humility and grace. I know that my career as an avant garde artist has been firmly launched. But I have to say something or I may seem arrogant.

Well, I learnt everything from my seniors in the field. I have only built a little bit on the rock foundation you all provided. And I am still learning from all of you, everyday…

Beneath the brilliance of the evening, I try to puzzle things out. How did I? I mean what exactly?

All I can remember of the previous evening is…I was stoned as hell when I did the damn painting. I started with a FEMALE body in mind. At some point I must have zoned out while continuing to work. When I came downstairs the next morning, I took one look at the lower half and said Bloody hell! How did THAT get there!

Seasonal Disorder

The comforting smell of Oliver's young and shiny fur calmed him to some extent but his irritation was not all gone. Both of them were used to these nightly sights and sounds from their humans' bedroom. On occasions like tonight when the door was open or ajar Oliver and Rex would be mute witnesses to the grunt-and-groan laden circus within. Invariably they would leave the spot in a minute or so, the departure prompted by sleepiness, boredom, disgust…all in varying orders.

As they settled into their warm doggie-beds under the stairs Rex growled in a tone that suggested the start of a long conversation.

You know…

Oliver sighed as quietly as he could because he knew the older dog was very sensitive.

(But Oliver tired …so tired…Oliver wants to sleep!)

Yes, Rex. I know.

Rex looked at him, his aged eyebrows twitching.

What do you know?

Oliver did a fake tail wag that said I still love you.

I know what you are going to say.

The twitching moved to the corner of the mouth. Oh dear…if Rex realized that Oliver was trying to shut him up, he would immediately take offense and wake the whole neighborhood up. Why do these older generation dogs have to be so loud about everything!

Look I was going to say…these humans try to train us. Sit here, not there. Get off the couch. Poo outside, not inside. Chew on this but not on anything else.

Okay so he wasn't offended. Oliver sighed in relief – loudly this time but it didn't matter because Rex, apart from being partially deaf, was immersed in his own tirade.

The worst part is all the rules about what to do and when.

You can't go outside, Rex it's too cold these days. No, Rex you HAVE to wear the pink sweater I knitted for you. It's a very bad winter this year.

We can't go to the park, Rex. Not now – look it's raining cats and dogs (which always makes me want to go out all the more! How many such cats I must have missed 'cause my human was afraid of a little rain!).

Come on Rex it's the first day of Spring, it's the best time for a walk. Now's not the time for sleeping! (But human, I want to sleep in today!)

Oliver's sighing was turning into gentle snoring. He knew the start, flow and end of Rex's speech like the back of his paw.

And yet, what about this? Rex went on.

Oh, wait, that's the beginning of the last paragraph. Quite a short speech today, really. Oliver cocked his ears and put on an expression of intense attention and adoration.

What about this noisy rough and tumble they do in bed that keeps us from our well-deserved sleep?

Rex turned to Oliver who was thankful he'd already put on the right expression.

Oliver, you talk to any of our normal friends – the horse on the neighboring farm, the visiting cat, the other dogs we meet, even the exotic ones we talk to at the zoo – all of God's NORMAL creatures have certain points in the year for this. Bloody humans are the only ones who are at it day in and day out! Including Sundays when even the Lord rested.

And they dare to teach me what to do and when. It's always not now, Rex. Now's not the right time, Rex. Later, Rex.

Unreasonable bastards!

*Or should I say…un-**seasonable** bastards?* He turned to Oliver with a grin.

Oliver smiled and grunted in sleepy approval, his loyalty to his old friend winning over his boredom at the same old joke.

A few minutes later one of the humans came downstairs for a drink of water. Both the dogs were curled up in deep slumber.

Awwwww, thought the human. *You guys are so cute.*

Darkness to light

I feel as ridiculous as I feel frightened. The solemn tones of the doctors, the never-ending smiles of people around me, the unnecessary hugs of colleagues at the store. Alright, alright! I don't need to understand all the medical terms to figure out that there's something terribly wrong with my brain.

Well, that's the scary part.

As for the ridiculous – well, right now in this position I can't help feeling like a character in a slapstick comedy – with half of me inside this strange machine (that I've seen only in medical dramas) and the other half sticking out! Like a clown in one of those silent era movies, half his person caught in something or the other, the other half struggling and making things worse – to the delight of the young ones in the cinema.

My top half – in the dark where I am subject to analysis but also, weirdly cocooned from the harsh light of reality. My bottom half – helplessly open to the glare of the world, waiting silently for news from the dark.

Mrs. Telovsky, how are you doing? Thank you for being patient. We're done now.

No. Leave me alone. I want to stay in the dark.

I feel my body slide out of the strange machine – and my mind slide into a pool of terror.

Here it comes. The light. The truth.

MEDICAL
REPORT

Know your neighbours

Long ago, when you said, *"Do you like cartoons? Come over!"* I didn't know that you'd be showing me other things too. I didn't know.

Long ago, when you told my parents, *"B seems to be a voracious reader…my library at home has lots of lovely books,"* I didn't know that some of those books weren't 'lovely' for a ten-year old. I didn't know.

Long ago, when you said, *"B adores Jackie Chan…you know what – I can teach B martial arts,"* we didn't know how much touching would be involved. We didn't know.

Long ago, when you told my parents, *"You guys enjoy your Sunday. I'll take B to the park,"* they didn't know that the park had dark and empty corners. They didn't know.

Long ago when schoolmates, cousins – and later colleagues and spouses – said, *"B's always moody or angry…best avoided!"* they didn't know that I was not to blame. They didn't know.

Yesterday when I visited you in the old age home and you said B, *would you be a sweetheart and bring me an iced tea* you didn't know what was in the tea. They didn't know either. I knew.

I knew.

Mid-career crisis

They look down on you if you don't have a successful career. They also disapprove if you've done too many things in your career. Too scattered a profile, I've heard my HR specialist friend say. Scattered, my foot!

I mean, look at me – I've been a plumber, au pair, chauffeur, electrician, psychologist, teacher and chef. Talk of jack-of-all-trades. And none of these jobs has made any difference to my bank balance!

I envy Nathan, wonderful man though he is. Masters in Financial Economics – and now he works for a bank. Focused, determined…and mainly, well paid.

Sigh!

MOM! Raoul hit his head on the old bookshelf again. I can see some blood… MOM! HURRY!

I'd better go.

Oh yeah, I forgot to add this to the list – first aid officer.

CHEF
CHAUFFEUR
TEACHER
PLUMBER
ELECTRICIAN
PSYCHOLOGIST
AU PAIR

Where the shoe pinches

"Oh, I wish all this stupid sand wouldn't keep getting inside me."

"Well, you can't have it all. At least Archie's sweaty feet are gone and there's a bit of a breeze."

"True. By the way, how you doing with the ingrown toenail these days?"

Shrugs. "Got used to it. Not as bad as when he wore the same socks for a week."

"Don't remind me. That was hell. I thought the two of us would be the first case of shoe suicide."

"You mean shoe-icide!"

"Please. Don't add your wordplay to the sand."

"Oh, and speaking of wordplay, have you noticed how so many of their expressions are insulting to us?"

"You mean like facial expressions? How can you see that high up?"

"No, I mean the way they talk."

"Oh, I see. Well, I'm still not sure what you mean."

"Okay when a human is called *a heel*, is it ever a compliment?"

"No."

"When they say *as common as an old shoe*, are they saying something nice about somebody?"

"No."

"How about *goody two-shoes*…are such people very popular?"

"No."

"*Quake in one's shoes* – negative emotion or positive?"

"Negative."

"*Shoe-string budget…* means what – luxurious holiday coming up?"

"Certainly not. And we've been on some of Archie's holidays!"

"See what I mean?"

"Hmm… You know I never really thought about it. How do you manage to see so many things that I completely miss?! Oh well, you know what they say about left-foot and right-foot shoes? The left-foot shoes are more analytical, more logical. That's you. I'm just a rightie!"

"Whatever, buddy. One thing's for sure. Political correctness in language just hasn't reached the upper regions. They have no clue, even in the 21st century."

"True…hey do you think all this will ever change? Will we, the shoes, ever stop being the underdogs?"

"Who knows? Maybe someday those science humans will develop a superior species, with the head at the bottom like it should be."

"That would be fun."

"Yes. Fun and correct. Order restored. The sky will truly be our limit then. And if it leads to a crisis the likes of Archie can think on their heads!"

Death is simple

It is, really.

They complicate it with the post-mortem, death certificate and other documents. But it's simply a question of a missing arm-nook for your head to move into at 2 am.

They complicate it with the legal will – if there is one – and what it entails. But it's simply a question of when, if ever, you find the will to get on with your life.

They complicate it with insurance policies and the final payout. But it's simply a question of the assurance that a familiar presence gave you at critical moments.

They complicate it with the funeral, memorials and many, many words. But it's simply a question of moving from a cooked dinner for two to a frozen meal for one.

They complicate it with relatives who suddenly visit, neighbors who suddenly wave and acquaintances who suddenly call. But it's simply a question of the mumbles through toothpaste foam and grunts through mists of sleep that you understood perfectly.

They complicate it with invitations to life-coach sessions and well-meant attempts to set you up. But it's simply a question of an armchair without the butt impression and half-done crossword you have known all your life.

They complicate it with bankers and lawyers explaining your future in fluent legalese. But, quite simply, it boils down to basic forms you meet on your own, with "married" and "single" boxes that make you wonder which one you are!

They complicate it with kids, friends and realtors assuring you that it is safer to live with lots of others in a retirement facility. But quite simply, it is not about how many others are present in your life, it is about the ONE who is missing.

RIP

One of us

Sweat circles marked his armpits, and if those weren't visible to you the dust and grime were evidence enough – this wasn't one of us. He didn't seem embarrassed or uneasy – in fact there was no indication that he felt anything at all, except for his darting glances towards the top-quality champagne that was flowing endlessly among the members of the club.

Sir Howard – as usual the first one to rise to action – gestured to Old Tom, the unofficial maître d'. Roused from his state of shock, that ancient member of the club gently floated across to the tramp and said, "I do believe you have lost your way…sir." (There was unmistakable irony in the "sir.") "Allow me to guide you to the door."

"Eh? Nah, nah, guv'nor. I'm no' lost…no' really. This *is* the righ' place. Coo, it's nice and warm in 'ere, innit?"

The maitre d' winced. Never, since his first day when he was taught the right angle at which to place the newspapers, had he heard such an accent in the hallowed club.

"I hardly think so." This time there was no "sir." "This is the venue of an important talk by Mr. William Carter, the famous sociologist from the University of …" Old Tom didn't see the point in explaining further and laid a ghost of a finger on the unfortunate intruder's sleeve.

"Yup, I knaow. Tha's me alrigh'. 'Cept that you go' a couple of de'ails wrong. Am a Socio*linguist*. And… ooh am doing a bi' of crowing now…it's *Doctor* William Carter…University of Aberdeen."

With that he moved to the podium, procuring a glass of champagne on the way with the grace of a ballerina. A couple of sips later, he addressed the august gathering in impeccable English, "Pardon me, ladies and gentlemen but I decided to conduct a little experiment before beginning my talk entitled" – he glanced at his papers – "Language and Social Class – Whither the Man on the Street?"

At that age

When Nurse came in, I was ready for her, though pretending to be asleep. As she checked my chart at the foot of the bed, I used my years of practice in the "10% open eyelids" to check out her full, firm figure.

"How long, do you think?"

Oh, so there were two of them today.

"You don't have to whisper, Maureen…he can't see or hear much. Any day, now. Poor man. He was a famous general, you know. I've seen his picture up on the wall at the War Museum. And now look at him. Just a frail eighty-four-year-old bag of bones."

As the first one picked up litter and an old medical bill or two from the floor, showing all kinds of lingerie, the second one reached over me to smooth the sheets near my pillow. Cleavage and some cheap perfume!

"Well, Sally, after a certain age it is downhill for all of us, I guess. You know how they say everything that goes up has to come down…that whole Newton, gravity thing? Well, it applies to life as well, I suppose."

As they left, I looked down at myself with a toothless grin. Does it really?

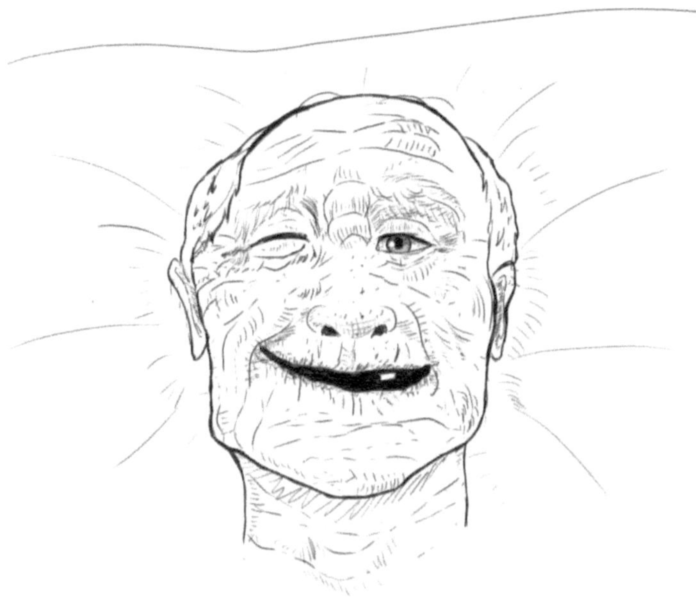

Decision

BEEP! SORRY. THE MAXIMUM CAPACITY HAS BEEN EXCEEDED.

JK Elevators! Who ever heard of such an elevator company? So weak — it can't even take 9 people! I did warn the building committee, you know.

Nobody was interested in Mr. Sinha's expert remarks.

BEEP! SORRY. THE MAXIMUM CAPACITY HAS BEEN EXCEEDED.

The young school girl was about to exit and take the stairs but she got a look from her mother that meant — *stay where you are, let someone else go.*

BEEP! SORRY. THE MAXIMUM CAPACITY HAS BEEN EXCEEDED.

Look, I'm late for a meeting. Can somebody please get out? Mr. Patel genuinely believed that his being the HR Manager at a medium-sized stationery business was what kept the world going.

Why don't YOU get out, Patel-ji? Shot back Archana, the gym instructor.

Well why don't YOU, Archana? You are young and fit. Just an observation but young people these days have no respect at all.

BEEP! SORRY. THE MAXIMUM CAPACITY HAS BEEN EXCEEDED.

Yes, Patel-ji we have often noticed your observation of the young and fit from your bedroom window.

Sniggers, a few quick looks at Patel, who immediately got engrossed in a detailed study of the floor of the elevator.

BEEP! SORRY. THE MAXIMUM CAPACITY HAS BEEN EXCEEDED.

Well, I'm not going. I single handedly managed the New Year party. I can't keep making sacrifices for the residents here. Shirley always had a ready reminder of her service-oriented soul.

Yes, Shirley. And we still have those unsettled questions about the New Year party expenses. Want to go over them one of these days? Das was still bitter that Shirley was on the party committee and he was not.

BEEP! SORRY. THE MAXIMUM CAPACITY HAS BEEN EXCEEDED.

Don't change the topic, Das. Why don't YOU leave the elevator? What's your excuse?

Well, the fact that I was the first to enter the elevator! I SHOULDN'T HAVE to leave.

Actually, uncle, we entered the elevator at the same time. But that's okay. I can leave.

Everybody was startled. As always Meera had managed to blend into the background and remain unnoticed…till she spoke.

Are you sure, Meera?

Oh yes. It's my day off. I'm in no hurry. I'll just wait for the elevator to come back.

Nobody spoke.

BEEP! SORRY. THE MAXIMUM CAPACITY HAS BEEN EXCEEDED.

Err…auntie, could you move a little…I'll get out…

So, Meera was serious about getting out. People made way to let her squeeze out of the eight-person box. It took a while, what with her bag, two mobiles, one crutch and one dysfunctional leg.

Once she was outside, the irritating electronic voice stopped, creating sufficient space for eight people and for a single thought that occupied all their minds – *how heartless these people are! What has become of our society!*

Meera smiled as society descended.

A flicker of light

When it is dark, really dark, I feel reassured. When there is no light to see by, the only vision is through the mind's eye. This means I have control over what I want to see – or at least it is easier to believe that I do.

The menacing heights of the ancient walls seem friendlier, the rough curtains of the austere abode seem smoother, the hard bed of the rustic chamber seem softer. It is easier to pray, easier to hope, easier to imagine that life was without its – very real – pain. In the stillness of the spartan room that has heard many a devout soul pour itself out in joy and agony, I feel safe.

But not for long.

Very soon the heavy steps of seniority

will be heard on the stairs.

Very soon the most revered soul of the order

will appear.

First the sound of ascent.

Then the smell of burning candles.

Slowly, the taste of fear that will choke me.

Finally, the light of the candle – as ruthless as the lust of its bearer.

And once my beloved darkness has surrendered to cruel light, the one missing sense – that of touch – will also arrive.

Up up team blue!

The excitement on the children's faces and in their voices was clear. It didn't really matter which team won – those few 'winning' kids would strut around with their team colors for a while but at the end of the day they'd ALL have had a happy day. Children never have egos large enough to interfere with pure fun. And Rita being by my side is a great help – she is a great assistant coach, in case there is any trouble.

All right kids – wear your colors straight; there should be no folds or wrinkles. See to it that your team leader is at the front of the line. Team Red – you lost points for forgetting that, last time. And Team Blue – you've been the winners for three weeks in a row but don't get over confident and don't even dream of sending Big Roy in first. I won't have him pushing smaller kids out of the way like last week.

Oh, well – I can't say they are NOT LISTENING but I can see that their patience is at an end. After all, they've heard these rules a hundred times before. And you can't really blame them – since the war began, these few moments of innocent fun is all they have. The army doesn't give us enough funds for a proper, age-appropriate saw or electric chair. These make-do arrangements are all we can do for these poor kids. As always, grownups start a war and children pay the price!

Right, get ready now. Our first prisoner is a big fat man from Annilistan. The cage will be lowered and opened in exactly one minute. Pick up your knives, shovels etc. No pushing, please. Remember, the extra points are for any team that gets a WHOLE organ – not a silly half-liver or a tiny slice of kidney. And Team Gold, I'm warning you – if you go straight for his eyes again, you'll be disqualified for three weeks. Remember Rule 112 of WHAT THE STATE SAYS ON FUN – the prisoner MUST BE ABLE TO SEE what is happening to his body till his last breath.

Right. Ready, get set…

TIME
FOR
GAMES!

A period in the future

2120 AD

A corporate building

As Jack weaved his way to an empty table in the office café Celine, Dina and Mariam exchanged quick glances with many meanings then looked down into their individual drinks.

Okay, he's gone. God, were you there at the meeting? He was as cranky as a sleepy toddler.

I know. It must be…you know…one of those days! (Expressive gesture that somehow manages to combine None-of-my-business with I'm-disgusted!)

But are you sure?

Oh, come on. We see it every month. It's like clockwork but on a monthly basis. Julius asks for a personal day, Geoff comes in looking annoyed with the whole world, Big Brad snaps at everybody…

True. And don't forget Colin's many trips to the bathroom.

Oh yes! You know, my husband is the same. Once I hear the mumbled words "Damn it I hate being male, it's a curse", I know that the next few days are going to be full of errands that I have to run and meals that I have to fix or order. As if my yoga, my book club and my time with my girlfriends aren't important at all. Every. Single. Month.

(Nods and gestures indicating "Exactly!")

And you're forgetting the main thing. You can't go anywhere NEAR them. For almost a week I lie in bed secretly wondering why my boyfriend is called Will. Is it short for William or Will Not?

(Laughter)

I do feel bad for them though. I mean if we had to go through something like that every month…and also manage a career, social commitments…such a balancing act can't be easy.

Okay, Celine, let me stop you right there. I agree that it's bad for them but that whole thing about the balancing act...well, nobody is asking them to balance anything! I mean this whole hiring more men to ensure gender balance is so messed up. Father Nature intended one half of humanity to stay at home. The men don't want to do that and then they expect all sorts of adjustments to be made by the rest of the world.

That's true, Dina. What was wrong with the way things were before? Before that damned Genders Law of...which year was it...2120? Now just look around you!

True. You know, I walked into the wrong washroom the other day — well of course when I started here there was only one kind of washroom — and I found these strange pot-like things lined up on the wall. I asked somebody and I believe they are for men to STAND and...oh, forget it! I just had lunch!

Oh yeah, we all heard about those. I mean okay so men's bodies are different from our normal ones but do we all have to see and know all these things?

Brief contemplative silence.

Oh well. Time to get back. And to circle back to what you said, Celine — don't get us wrong. We're all for helping, supporting men but some things are just not for us to handle.

Exactly. Don't bother us with all the unnecessary stuff! I mean there's a reason why they don't call it WOMENstruation!

(Laughter)

Anticipation

When they say war changes everything, they probably don't mean THIS personal, THIS intimate level of change. A person's mental images being replaced by new ones that are similar (but so dissimilar), in a process that feels so real that it was like the individuals themselves were reaching within to pluck out pictures and implant new ones! Do war experts have a technical term for this?!

As Mercia waited for Viktor – her dear Viky – to arrive from across the border, one of the first lucky ones to benefit from the long-awaited end to three decades of bloodshed, she struggled to keep the original images in her mind in place and unchanged.

Her favorites were the worst affected. A clear image of her and Viky surrounded by flags, streamers, dresses and flowers all in shades of purple to mark the victory of a sports team they both loved…had now turned into a melancholic tableau with smoke, corpses and debris and splashed all over with only red – the deep red of congealed blood.

A scene of pure joy – she walking along their favorite spot on the river, quite annoyed that he was late and Viky hiding behind a bush waiting to throw a rose at her as she passed – had remolded itself into a grim spectacle – a soldier on patrol, not suspecting a thing and a sniper behind a bush, taking aim.

An intimate picture of their two bodies bathed in love and sweat, each struggling to prolong the other's pleasure…was gone. And in its place was a very public picture of two male bodies bathed in hate and blood, each struggling to do away with the other before the other did it to him!

Mercia shuddered, shook her head and secretly looked down at her shoulders hoping to see bits and pieces of the wrong colors and wrong pictures thrown out by her mind.

"This is not a wedding album that some disgruntled spouse can disfigure!" she muttered to herself. "These mental images are all I have, for God's sake! They have kept me alive for thirty years, kept my faith in the knowledge that Viky and I being from enemy countries did not matter! Why are they taking these new, horrible forms now?"

As Mercia heard with sudden joy the sound of the army trucks – as the waves of excitement and anticipation swept through the waiting crowds – she was paralyzed by a sudden thought. What about the images in HIS mind? Were they the same? Had they changed too?

Summoned by the principle

A TUESDAY MORNING, JULY 1988

10 AM

I wasn't sure what sort of stand my parents would take. They had never been summoned to the principal's office before. I wasn't good at Math and I hated Geography but overall, they had heard only "good things" about my performance at school. But today was different.

The rickety fan tried very hard to cool the room and soothe the tension – succeeding in neither. My class teacher was frowning – not her usual permanent frown but something more serious, specially ordered for me and for today. The principal, as always, had a blank expression – though even that was usually enough for most of us! And I…I just stood there experiencing a strange combination of fear and defiance.

The piece de resistance of this little drama was a sheet of paper with my handwriting on it. It moved from the desk to the hands of the two esteemed educators as they read, mulled over, lip-chewed at and generally treated it like it was a severed thumb from a crime scene.

11 AM

It had been about twenty minutes since my parents arrived. Amma was worried but my dad had that twinkle in his eye that told me that, despite his nodding at everything the school was telling him, he didn't think I was at fault.

The words in the room washed over me in a surreal way…

…only eleven years old…

…spoiling the other, innocent…

…how does he even know about…

…who actually wrote this?

…what kind of exposure are you giving your…

11.10 AM

Alright, madam. We'll speak to our son at home. But tell me, you asked a Year 6 student to write an essay on Mother Nature and he began with… (reading from the paper)

Just say Nature! Nature can't be a mother. Nature makes women menstruate and men go scot-free. What kind of mother does that to her daughters?

What he has written may be silly but perhaps our son is ahead of his class in his thinking — and perhaps ahead of his teachers in his approach. Do you want to punish him for this?

I can't remember the educators' response to this. Not because all this was thirty-four years ago, but because they didn't have any.

ANOTHER TUESDAY MORNING, JULY 2022

I realized today that my lifelong lessons in language, gender studies and the meaning of parenting and education perhaps began that morning.

PRINCIPAL

Royalty and nobility

> Xavier let out a sigh that was felt, more than heard, by the others. The walls of the conference room seemed to scream "YOU BASTARDS! DO YOU REALIZE THE SIZE OF HIS SACRIFICE, THE NOBILITY OF HIS DECISION? DON'T YOU SEE THE INJUSTICE BEING DONE TO SOMEONE WHO HAS ALWAYS BEEN AN UPRIGHT CITIZEN, A MODEL HUMAN BEING, THE SALT OF THE EARTH IN EVERY SENSE?"

Of course, they were only walls. Who cares about walls?

As Anita left the table with her notebook still open, she thought, "That's it! Just a couple of lines to give it a well-rounded ending – those always come to me like magic after my afternoon nap. And I'll type it all up before dinner."

At lunch, Anita wondered if she had made Xavier, her protagonist, rather weak – well going by what a "hero" is expected to be. "But that's just it," she muttered. "A hero and a protagonist are not the same! It's up to the readers to understand that!"

Her muttering continued with her post-lunch cigarette.

"Literature needs its upstanding citizens, its moral beings, its Xaviers! There has been too much of all that anti-hero stuff, all the flimsily constructed sensational paperbacks…and those overnight successes who call themselves writers – do they truly understand the art? Do they have any idea of the damage that such writing can have on future generations – hell, on the CURRENT generation?"

Anita's vision of herself as a writer was different! "Literature has its higher purpose – to edify, to elevate, to enable the building of a better human community; to be a firm but fair social critic. A large, clean and bold mirror reflecting the minds of people. What was it Sir Philip Sydney said – literature should delight and instruct! Well, she was going to do just that! She was…

(Tring Tring!) Anita walked to the phone, balancing a lowly cigarette and lofty thoughts.

"Hello? Hey, Matthew! Oh yes, it's done; I'll send it across tomorrow morning."

(Listening)

"Yeah, it took a while but I think you'll like the ending. Worth the long wait, I promise you."

(Listening)

"You bloody what? No effing way, Matthew! This is the second time you're trying this crap. Don't you dare play around with my contract. Senior Editor be damned, you're a dishonest piece of shit, Matthew! New publishing policy, my ass! You think I don't know what that means financially? Listen you lousy old weasel – I've been with you thirteen years. That's seven best sellers I have given your firm. And I'm not doing it to secure a place in heaven – I do it for my royalty cheques! If I get one cent less than what I should be getting, I'm changing publishers! Don't you even dream of…"

As the tirade went on Anita didn't notice the ash from her cigarette falling on the open page, where her protagonist, Xavier the upright, was still sighing.

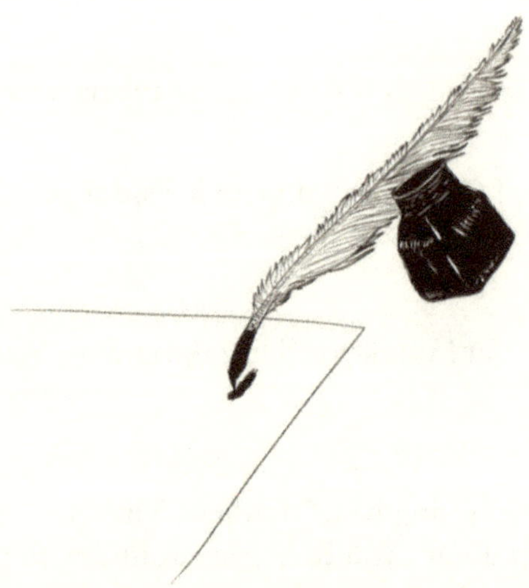

Seeing and unseeing

The eyes follow me everywhere, tracking me as I go about my chores. Tracking the ordinariness of my "decent" mornings, before the school bus arrives. Later, tracking the men who come and go, come and go.

Sometimes I feel for the eyes – the only mobile part of that body now. When the rest of it moved I had only pain. Every kind of pain. For seven years.

Sometimes the eyes seem to want to fill me with guilt. When I sense that, I punish them…by handling my business in the same room, making them watch. With only a night lamp on, the men never realize they have a captive audience. Or that the vague shape in the dark isn't just a pile of clothes.

Later, bare-bodied, I stare into the eyes mockingly. Not because I want to see the impotent lust in them. But because I want them to see the unfading traces of the first seven years. The old bruises, scars, burn marks. Then the eyes move in terror to the heavy marble statuette in the corner. The one that came handy when I decided that enough was enough.

Someday the scars on my body will fade…and forgive. But only the scars on my body.

Had I known...

It didn't matter to me that you and I were the same color – brown. Actually no, it did matter. It irked me that based on that one linking factor between us you assumed an unnecessary familiarity with me. Yes, I wasn't an Arab or a Westerner but somebody from the same subcontinent as you. But I was Manager and you, Cleaner. I sat at a desk with a computer; I organized and chaired meetings; I coordinated courses for senior officers of the Home Ministry. You cleaned toilets.

I had noticed early on that as you spoke no Arabic or English, communication with you was a Herculean task and I helped you (and the others) using the one common language we have. That was a mistake. There is a difference between a helping hand and a hand of friendship.

I tried to indicate my disapproval of the way you frequently walked into my office and struck up a conversation with me. I was not your peer or friend. I was one of the senior-most employees in the organization. I took no or very little notice of the pics of your family that you shoved under my nose. I brushed off many an attempt on your part to start a casual chat – most often because I was genuinely pressed for time, but also because I didn't think it was right. I snubbed you. You missed that and persisted. I couldn't believe that somebody could be so daft.

On Thursday morning when you made a stupid mistake with the cleaning, I just lost it. Nobody really cared how much or how loudly I yelled at you because in their inability to communicate with you, over a few months you had ceased to exist for them. My yelling being all in English, you just stood there gaping at me like a fish watching a horror movie, as though keeping your mouth wide open would enable you to swallow some of the tirade, for later mastication.

By the time the kitchen staff told me that the cleaning that morning had been done by somebody else (not you), you had disappeared into the laborers' bus.

By the time the security told me that you were at the clinic and HR all morning, I was getting into the car to go home.

By the time I heard over the weekend that the Covid wave was costing people their jobs, affecting about fifty people on the campus with immediate effect, the entire memory of that morning had been replaced by more important things.

By the time I heard the following week that you were among the fifty unlucky ones, you weren't coming into work anymore.

Had I known that morning that it was the last time I was seeing you I would have yelled less or not at all.

Had I known that morning that it was your last day I would have asked whose "fault" it was and if yours, taken it easy.

Had I known last week that you were getting fired I would have had a long chat with you.

Had I known over the months that you were soon to be sacked I would have spurned you LESS often and recalled MORE often that I too was once a lost person in a foreign country.

Had I but known…

Afternoon walk

Sometimes the glare is so strong that one has to walk not just with the head covered, but the entire face. Thankfully in a desert village where hardly anybody ventures out at this point in the afternoon it doesn't matter. There is nobody and nothing to bump into. Vast masses of sand, a few scraggly bushes and the odd bunch of huts, as stark in their poverty as in their sun-bakedness.

Unaware of the sour smell from a drenched body that had never seen a deodorant, unaware of the cruel arrogance of the sun, unaware of the steam rising from the few, very few proper roads in the area, unaware of how far she was getting from her construction site, unaware of her hunger pangs, she walks on…aware, only of the gradually dwindling distance between herself and the two-room school she was heading towards.

There it is, the building that holds under its roof the education of many age groups, the future of many families and – in its ricketiness, the promises of many politicians. As she ignores the leer of the sleepy watchman-cum-cleaner and walks towards the noisy classroom, she stops for a minute to catch her breath and what little dignity she has left in life.

Having approached the table which bears the burden of books, chalk and the feet of the sleeping teacher, she whispers, "Master-ji!" She is torn between the sacrilege of arousing this grand educator from his slumber and her very real need to get back to the construction site – a delay in which means less wages to take home or a bribe to the supervisor after dusk (in kind but most unkind).

"Master-ji!" She decides to be louder and risk the wrath of her son's teacher. The irritated teacher looks up from his sleep, stares for a few seconds and then looks at the sign on the wall announcing the last date for paying fees. Finally comprehending the mystery of the situation, he takes the money from her and writes out a barely decipherable receipt. As he gives it to her, he lightly presses her palm with the tips of his fingers. She is a widow after all and belongs to the poorest section of the village. That lot is always desperate for money – you never know when you get lucky with their women! Being a teacher, he obviously believed in life-long learning and exploring every possible opportunity for self-development. Like a chance with this woman.

Ignoring – or perhaps unaware of – the teacher's attempt, she walks out of the schoolroom, carefully avoiding looking at her son in order to save him unnecessary embarrassment and teasing. As she surveys the vast, hot yellow-brownness of the distance back to the construction site she has visions. Not the usual hallucinatory effects of heat stroke so common in the region. These were gentler, cooler and more pleasant…and involved her old age when she would finally be 'retired' and under the care of her educated, well-employed son.

Transit

I am in transit and the connecting flight is delayed. Interesting – this is the third time in two years that my time at a transit airport is unexpectedly stretched. I have tried my best to avoid stupid interpretations and silly symbolistic theories but this is the third time! Why shouldn't I believe that this is reflective of my own life – an ever changing but never forming entity, a six-footer of a person who has the same characteristics as an amoeba – a sense of shapelessness, cellular singularity and unending de- and re-formation!

I try to avoid the men's washroom – my bladder can wait till I am on the flight. After all, my bladder has been quite mature about its new neighbors in the large compound that is my body.

Also, I am not sure if the men's is where I should "go" anymore.

On the other hand, I glance at the silhouette on the door of the women's washroom and I am not sure if that is me either.

This is just like my childhood in an army officer's family – with mom getting new postings every three years we were never in a place that was "home." But then I wouldn't have been "home" if we'd lived on the same street for twenty years! My confused sense of Am-I-home? was internal. My own body and mind didn't feel at home with each

other. The changes in the one and the longings in the other were –
forget at home – not even in the same town.

So here I am at thirty-seven, relieved of all my savings in what they
claimed was a life-changing surgery, standing between two countries,
two flights, two washrooms and at least two groups of "normal"
people – the one's subtle glances of curiosity and the other's open
words of mirth were both familiar. The only question is – where is the
life-changing bit?

Okay, that's my flight, finally! I hope I don't get a middle seat. It is so
rare in life that I am firmly on THIS or THAT side of anything!

As I pick up my bags, I think of the airport signs again. TRANSIT next
to TRANSFER. Sometimes when you transit, your problems merely
get transferred – they don't go away.

In a way society is like an amoeba too…but with more de-formation
and very little reformation.

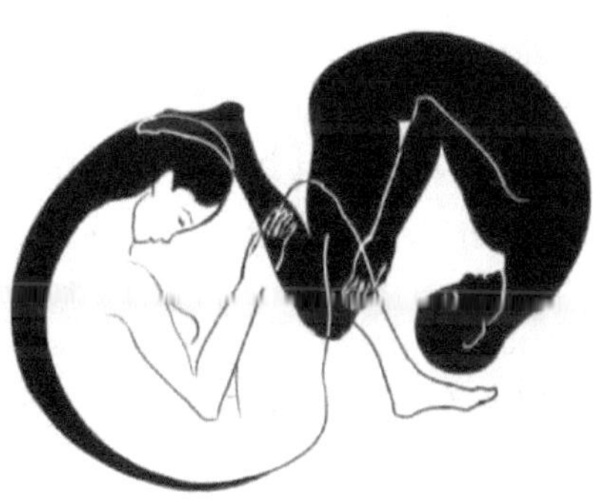

Nursery rhyme on a couch

The embarrassed silence was broken only by the pen-clicking of the esteemed psychiatrist. I had to struggle to rein in a chuckle – all those months on his couch had no impact on me…but it had definitely broken him!

Hump. He said HUMP, the dignified three piece-suited, letter opener-using, stuffy old gentleman. He usually said, "Err…you know, physical relations," or "When you were…errmm…intimate with her." He wouldn't even say "sex." And today he just lost it and said, *"You mean right after you humped and dumped her AND her sister!"* Ha-ha! Is he going to use the F-word next week?

However, on the whole his analysis of my problem made sense. I mean I've been subjected to all kinds of silly rhymes that children usually are – by parents, teachers and later, sticky little nephews and nieces. Why had this one alone become an unstoppable earworm, tormenting me day in and day out, so much so that I had to seek professional help?

So now I have the answers. The wall is my habit of never letting anybody get close. The horses and men are my true friends and well-wishers who tried their best to help. But I failed them all. I was content – or so I thought – in a long, unending series of sexual "conquests." I was addicted to the series because some part of me felt that I was restoring justice for the trauma of my childhood by seducing, humping…and dumping women.

The doc was right. I AM humpty-dumpty.

The bored room

They come and go.

Managers and damagers. Executives and executioners. People in assistant roles and people in asinine roles

Human resources and inhuman practices. Surging professional lives and suffering personal lives.

I take note of the baggage they bring. Not just the sleek briefcases and monogrammed bags but the less glamorous, more human piles of ego, insecurity, jealousy and prejudice.

I see them disregard the (inner) environment with their use-and-throw plastic smiles.

I hear the pretend tones and over-friendly conversations that made masks a normal thing long before theater or pandemics did.

I watch the presentations that present representations of presents (only for the management!) – in the present and beyond!

I admire the tenacity of those who finish the race and sympathize with those who fall and never get up…and laugh at the naivete of the "winners" who think the race is – ever – finished.

I marvel at how literary scholars have missed out by not acknowledging an important genre of our times – management speak.

I look on as allies meet and part, as friends and foes merge those dividing lines into an amoebic amalgam of any-time alteration.

I bear witness to secret exchanges of collegial smiles that combine the thrill of adventure with the guilt of adultery.

I observe the invisible pursing of lips and sharp glances as people with attractive figures sense unwelcome, lingering looks.

I read over shoulders as they strategize the best ways to prove the diverse and open-minded culture of the company even as I read their secret thoughts at how a tiny Vietnamese woman named Tam could possibly bag the important business deal or why the blacks couldn't stick to sports or music.

I am the boardroom, ever alert, accommodating of a range of employed entities.

I am also the bored room, never impressed, disapproving of a range of embedded frailties.

Please sir, can I have some more?

The waiter knew I was the odd one in the group. I had tried my best – borrowed Linda's shiny shoes, polished my old purse till the cracks were hardly visible, skipped lunch to get the "extra special dry clean" for my only decent dress. I had pored over the pages from old women's magazines that had almost replaced the peeling wallpaper of my sad room, in an attempt to arrive at a combination of expensive-looking-but-not-expensive, for my make-up. I had ignored my own friends and tried my best to listen in on 'their' conversations – what the rich girls talked about, the fashionable terms they used and how to say them as if I belonged! I had practiced walking with the "air" that seemed to come so easily to them, despite my best friend's gleeful remark that I might as well put on a price tag and walk up and down Main Street after dark!

But the moment I appeared at the entrance of St. George's Hotel I knew it was over. How did they know? How *do* they know? The doorman stooped, pretending to pick up something just as I reached the door. The lady with the reservations said, *"Oh you're with the Paltridges group. This way, please"* in a tone that hinted very softly that she actually meant *"What are YOU doing with the Paltridges group?"* The liveried footman pulled back the chair to seat me but made me feel less like a guest at a fancy restaurant and more like a person in a wheelchair with a nurse who hadn't been paid for a year.

I guess they are justified in a way. Power by proximity, I suppose. Being in the presence of so many important people every day gives them a false sense of their own increased importance. And behind the immaculate uniforms and perfectly choreographed grace and finery, I am sure they are treated like rubbish by their overlords. So, when they find a guest who they instinctively recognise as 'one of us among some of them' they see a victim on whom their frustration can be dumped!

Great, now this! Twice the wine glasses were refilled – all the glasses except mine! And the skipping was done with such an easy expertise that I almost admired him for it – *nobody* noticed it and if they did, they'd never believe that it was deliberate. Do the waiters at such places get special training in being rude to people who "don't belong to the right set?" Probably yes, as the establishment would like to keep the wrong set out!

Anyway. The great war was over and the upper classes needed to realize that their world is crumbling. Working class girls like me had to speak up. My heart was racing with indignation and fear. I knew it was easier to make my peace but I also knew it was nobler to fight. And if there was going to be a scene, good! It was a message not just to this rude waiter but to their whole snobbish world! I mentally tried out a tone that was ironically, sarcastically polite.

"Ahem! Please, sir!"

About the Author

Kiran.R

Kirankumar Ramachandran studied English and Comparative Education at the Universities of Madras and Oxford. He is currently on a doctoral journey exploring language and gender. His love affair with creative writing started with "the most horrible teenage poems, worse than acne," moved on to slightly more mature short stories, plots of novels (never written) and has finally reached what he calls his comfort space – flash/very short fiction. He develops English courses for the Police department in Qatar where he lives with his wife Ruchita, his collection of bells and masks and hundreds of books of which he keeps reading the same few again and again.

He can be reached at *kkeducare@gmail.com*